S0-ADP-569

Joseph
Virginia
32815

DATE DUE

1998	

PRINTED IN U.S.A.

The United States

Virginia

Paul Joseph
ABDO & Daughters

visit us at
www.abdopub.com

Published by Abdo & Daughters, 4940 Viking Drive, Suite 622, Edina, Minnesota 55435.
Copyright © 1998 by Abdo Consulting Group, Inc., Pentagon Tower, P.O. Box 36036,
Minneapolis, Minnesota 55435 USA. International copyrights reserved in all countries.
No part of this book may be reproduced in any form without written permission from the
publisher.

Printed in the United States.

Cover and Interior Photo credits: Peter Arnold, Inc., SuperStock, Archive

Edited by Lori Kinstad Pupeza
Contributing editor Brooke Henderson
Special thanks to our Checkerboard Kids—Jack Ward, Stephanie McKenna,
Priscilla Cáceres, Matthew Nichols

All statistics taken from the 1990 census; The Rand McNally Discovery Atlas of The
United States.

Library of Congress Cataloging-in-Publication Data

Joseph, Paul 1970-
     Virginia / Paul Joseph.
     p. cm. -- (United States)
     Includes index.
     ISBN 1-56239-889-X
     1. Virginia--Juvenile literature. I. Title. II. Series: United States (Series)
     F226.3.J67   1998
     975.5--dc21
                                              97-34109
                                          CIP
                                          AC

Contents

Welcome to Virginia

Virginia lies on the eastern coast of the United States. Although it sits in the middle of the east coast, it is called the Old South. Virginia is shaped roughly like a triangle. It **borders** the Atlantic Ocean for 112 miles (180 km).

The state has some of the most beautiful land in the country. It is loaded with mountains, valleys, national forests, rolling hills, and a wonderful coast.

The state of Virginia is well known for its role in shaping American history. In 1607, the first lasting settlement in America was set up on its shores. In 1619, Jamestown, Virginia, was the meeting place for the first representatives forming the **government** of America.

As one of the 13 original states, Virginia continued to play a large role in the leadership of the country. Two of the greatest wars fought in the United States came to a close in Virginia. In both of these wars, people from Virginia helped fight in and end the war.

Virginia's nickname is the Old Dominion State. The state would later earn the nickname Mother of Presidents because of the outstanding number of Virginians who became presidents of the United States. Virginia produced four of the first five presidents, and later would produce an additional four.

Allegheny Mountains in Virginia.

Fun Facts

VIRGINIA

Capital
Richmond (203,056 people)
Area
39,700 square miles
(102,823 sq km)
Population
6,216,568 people
Rank: 12th
Statehood
June 25, 1788
(10th state admitted)
Principal rivers
James River, Potomac River,
Rappahannock River
Highest point
Mount Rogers;
5,729 feet (1,746 m)
Largest city
Virginia Beach (393,069 people)
Motto
Sic semper tyrannis
(Thus always to tyrants)
Song
"Carry Me Back to Old Virginia"
Famous People
Ella Fitzgerald, Patrick Henry,
Thomas Jefferson, Robert E. Lee,
James Madison, James Monroe,
Booker T. Washington, George
Washington

Virginia is one of the original 13 colonies

13

*D*ogwood Flower

*S*tate Flag

*D*ogwood

*C*ardinal

About Virginia

The Old Dominion State

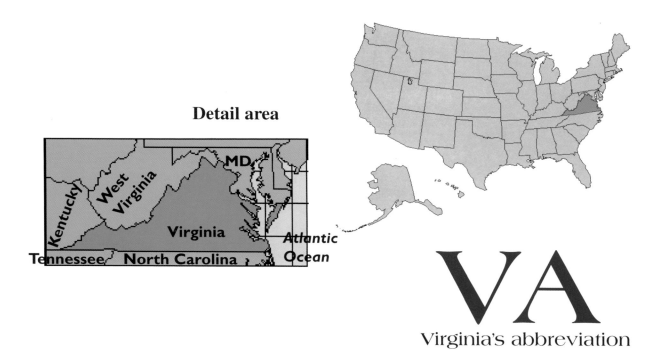

Detail area

Kentucky
West Virginia
MD
Virginia
Atlantic Ocean
Tennessee
North Carolina

VA

Virginia's abbreviation

Borders: west (Kentucky, West Virginia), north (West Virginia, Maryland), east (Maryland, Atlantic Ocean), south (Tennessee, North Carolina)

Nature's Treasures

The beautiful state of Virginia has many treasures in its state. There are thick forests, scenic mountains, pretty valleys, sandy beaches, fertile soil, and excellent **grazing** land for animals.

The thick forests in the state have many different kinds of trees in them. Some that can be found are pine and hardwood. Forests can be found in the mountain regions and the lowlands. Some of these forests are national and state parks, which make for great hiking and camping.

The mountains of Virginia are also wonderful sites. The most famous mountains in the state are the Blue Ridge Mountains.

People enjoy swimming, boating, skiing, and fishing in the Atlantic Ocean. There are many **fisheries** in the state. Some of the fish caught off the Virginia coast include, flounder, croaker, oysters, and blue crabs.

The land is excellent for farming. Tobacco has always been one of the most valuable crops grown in the state. Other crops grown are soybeans, corn, peanuts, and wheat. In the southwestern part of Virginia, animals use the land to **graze**.

Under the ground, **minerals** can be found. Some of the minerals found in the state are coal, stone, and sand.

Sandy beaches of Virginia.

Beginnings

In 1607, King James I of England, sent three ships filled with **settlers** over to America. These settlers landed in what is now Virginia and set up an English settlement in America. They named this settlement Jamestown for their King.

When these English settlers landed in Virginia, many **Native Americans** already were living in the area. Throughout the 1600s many wars broke out between the new settlers and the Native Americans over land. By the late 1600s, the settlers had taken over most of the land.

As the years went by, the settlers were becoming wealthy tobacco farmers. However, these farmers were paying a lot of money to the English **government**. This is known as taxes. Virginia, along with the rest of America, wanted their freedom from England. This is when the **American Revolution** started.

After many bloody battles, America won the war. On June 25, 1788, Virginia became the 10th state. Less than 100 years later, Virginia left the United States and joined the **Confederacy** in 1861.

The **Civil War** was between the northern states and the southern states. The southern states were known as the Confederacy. The Confederacy wanted to keep slaves as workers on their farms. The North, however, wanted to stop slavery because it was cruel.

After many battles, the North finally won the Civil War and slavery was ended. In 1870, Virginia and the rest of the South again became part of the United States.

The fall of Richmond, Virginia, during the Civil War.

B.C. to 1693

Early Land and Settlements

During the Ice Age, many thousands of years ago, Virginia was covered by ice and glaciers. Later the ice began to melt and the land of Virginia began to form.

The first known people to live in and have settlements in Virginia are the **Native Americans**.

1607: Jamestown is founded in Virginia. It is the first long-lasting English settlement in North America.

1693: The College of William and Mary was started in Williamsburg. It is the second college started in the United States.

Virginia

B.C. to 1693

1716 to 1789

Statehood and More

1716: The first theater in the United States is built in Williamsburg.

1776: Virginia, along with the rest of America, declares its independence from England.

1788: Virginia becomes the 10th state on June 25.

1789: George Washington, born in 1732, near Oak Grove, Virginia, becomes the first president of the United States.

Virginia

1716 to 1789

1861 to Present

Modern Virginia

1861: Virginia leaves the Union to join the **Confederacy**. Richmond, Virginia, is named the Confederate capital.

1870: After the Confederacy surrenders to the Union, Virginia rejoins the Union.

1952: The John H. Kerr Dam on Roanoke River is completed.

1985: Terrible floods follow hurricane Juan.

1990: L. Douglas Wilder is sworn in as **governor** of Virginia. He is the first elected African American governor in the United States.

Virginia

1861 to Present

Virginia's People

There are about 6.2 million people living in the state of Virginia. It is the 12th largest state in the country.

Many well-known people have come from Virginia. The state is known as the Mother of Presidents for its many presidents. Eight presidents were from Virginia.

George Washington is the most famous president and person to come from Virginia. He is known as "the Father of the Country," for being the first president of the United States.

The country's third, fourth, and fifth presidents were also from Virginia. They were Thomas Jefferson, James Madison, and James Monroe.

Four other presidents also made Virginia home. They were William Henry Harrison, the 9th president. John Tyler, the 10th president. Zachary Taylor, the 12th president, and Woodrow Wilson, the 28th president.

Other famous people from Virginia are L. Douglas Wilder. The grandson of slaves, Wilder became the first black **governor** ever in the United States.

Actor Warren Beatty, Actress Shirley MacLaine, and Hall of Fame Quarterback Fran Tarkenton are all from Virginia.

George Washington

L. Douglas Wilder

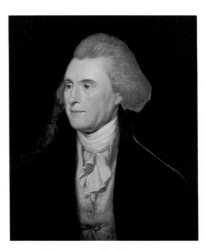

Thomas Jefferson

Splendid Cities

Virginia has many splendid cities in its state with many things to do and see. People from Virginia live in both large and small cities.

The largest city in the state is Virginia Beach. It has many **resorts** on the Atlantic Ocean where **tourists** go to have fun. The city has sandy beaches, great fishing, and nice golf courses. State Parks, fine museums, other entertainment add to this fine city.

Virginia's second largest city is Norfolk. It is a port city where the James River enters the Chesapeake Bay. It is an excellent area for both **military** naval and air bases. The college, Old Dominion University, is in Norfolk.

Arlington

Richmond

Roanoke

Norfolk

Virginia Beach

The third largest city and the state capital of Virginia is Richmond. Richmond is one of the leading **industrial** cities of the South. There are wonderful museums in Richmond, which include the Edgar Allen Poe Museum and the Virginia Museum of Fine Arts.

Other splendid cities in Virginia include Newport News, Chesapeake, Hampton, Arlington, Portsmouth, and Roanoke, to name a few.

Virginia Beach, Virginia.

Virginia's Land

Virginia has some of the most beautiful land in the country. There are mountains, forests, lakes, rivers, and valleys. The state's land is divided into five different regions.

The Coastal Plain region covers all of the eastern part of Virginia. Besides being right on the ocean, this region also has the Potomac, York, and James rivers. This low land has a lot of swampy and wet areas.

The Piedmont Plateau region lies west of the Coastal Plain in the middle of Virginia. This region is filled with low rolling hills.

The Blue Ridge region runs through

the entire state. In the north the Potomac and Shenandoah rivers join to cut a deep notch through the Blue Ridge Mountains. The highest point in the state is in this region. Mount Rogers is 5,729 feet (1,746 m) tall.

The Valley and Ridge region covers most of western Virginia. Its greatest feature is the Shenandoah Valley. The limestone soil of this valley make it excellent for farming and growing crops.

The Appalachian Plateau region covers a very small part of western Virginia. The streams of this region have created a maze of deep ravines and winding ridges.

Wild horses grazing in Virginia's sand dunes.

Virginia at Play

The people of Virginia and the many people who visit the state have a lot of things to do and see. For many years **tourists** have enjoyed the historic sites, beaches, mountains, and national parks of Virginia.

Many visitors to the state enjoy the wonderful 105-mile (169-km) route through Skyline Drive and the Blue Ridge Parkway on the top of the western mountains. People like to stop and take pictures of the scenic views.

Because Virginia has such a rich historic tradition, tourists often come to see the museums and historic landmarks. People can see the battlefields of the **American Revolution** and the **Civil War**.

Tourists also visit the homes of such American figures as presidents Washington, Jefferson, Monroe, and Wilson. Many people come to the state to see the historic cities of Jamestown and Williamsburg.

The beautiful outdoors of Virginia have parks, clear lakes and rivers, and the sandy beaches of the Atlantic Ocean.

Thomas Jefferson's home in Charlottsville, Virginia.

Virginia at Work

The people of Virginia must work to make money. At one time, farming was Virginia's leading **industry**. Today it is **manufacturing**.

The largest business in Virginia is making chemicals and medicine. Others are shipbuilding, and making electric and electronic parts.

About one out of every five people working in Virginia work for the **government**. Most of the federal workers in Virginia have jobs in Washington, D.C.

When Virginia was first becoming a state, most jobs centered around farming. The most valuable crop then was tobacco. Today, tobacco still is one of the leading crops of the state. Others include soybeans, corn, peanuts, wheat, and potatoes.

Some people in Virginia are **miners**. Virginia is one of the top 10 coal-mining states in the country. Other people in Virginia work in **fisheries** on the coast.

Virginia offers many different things to do and see. Because of its natural beauty, people, land, coast, and history, the state of Virginia is a great place to visit, live, work, and play.

Shipbuilding in Virginia.

Fun Facts

• Besides Virginia being known as the "Mother of Presidents," it is also known as the "Mother of States." Eight other states were created from Virginia's original land.

• Virginia's most eastern land is on a **peninsula**. This peninsula is called Delmarva Peninsula. The name was formed from letters of the three states that are on this peninsula. They are Delaware, Maryland, and Virginia.

• Virginia had two capitals before its present capital of Richmond. They are Jamestown and Williamsburg. Richmond has been the capital since 1780.

Children playing on a beach in Virginia.

Glossary

American Revolution: a war that gave the United States its independence from Great Britain.

Border: the edge of something, the edge of a state.

Civil War: a war between groups within the same country.

Confederacy: a group that bands together for a common belief. In this case it is the 11 southern states that left the Union between 1860 and 1861.

Fisheries: the business of catching fish.

Government: working for the country, state, city, or county.

Governor: the highest elected official in the state.

Graze: animals eating grass.

Industrial: big businesses such as factories or manufacturing.

Manufacture: to make things by machine in a factory.

Minerals: things found in the earth, such as rock, diamonds, coal, etc.

Miners: people who work underground to get minerals.

Military: working within the armed forces, such as the army or navy.

Native Americans: the first people who were born in and occupied North America.

Peninsula: a long narrow piece of land that extends into the water.

Population: the number of people living in a certain place.

Resort: a place to vacation that has fun things to do.

Settlers: people that move to a new land where no one has lived before and build a community.

Tourists: people who travel for pleasure.

Internet Sites

Virginia an Internet Tour
http://www.rivnet.net/riv61.htm
This page consists of links to places of interest in Virginia.

Virginia
http://dit1.state.va.us/
The Commonwealth of Virginia is a state of rich heritage and extraordinary natural beauty. Its attractions are as broad and diverse as its geography and as abundant as its history. Stretching from the Atlantic Ocean to the Blue Ridge and Allegheny mountains, Virginia is a mixture of exciting cities, historic towns, plentiful resources, and a wealth of recreational activities.

These sites are subject to change. Go to your favorite search engine and type in Virginia for more sites.

PASS IT ON

Tell Others Something Special About Your State

To educate readers around the country, pass on interesting tips, places to see, history, and little unknown facts about the state you live in. We want to hear from you!

To get posted on ABDO & Daughters website, e-mail us at "mystate@abdopub.com"

Index